Careers in Construction

General Contractor

Pete Schauer

Cavendish Square

New York

Published in 2016 by Cavendish Square Publishing, LLC
243 5th Avenue, Suite 136, New York, NY 10016

First Edition

Website: cavendishsq.com

This publication represents the opinions and views of the author based on his or her personal
experience, knowledge, and research. The information in this book serves as a general guide only.
The author and publisher have used their best efforts in preparing this book and disclaim liability
rising directly or indirectly from the use and application of this book.

CPSIA Compliance Information: Batch #CW16CSQ

All websites were available and accurate when this book was sent to press.

Library of Congress Cataloging-in-Publication Data

Names: Schauer, Peter J., author.
Title: General contractor / Pete Schauer.
Description: New York: Cavendish Square Publishing, [2016] | Series: Careers
in construction | Includes bibliographical references and index.
Identifiers: LCCN 2015034151 | ISBN 9781502609786 (library bound)
| ISBN 9781502609793 (ebook)
Subjects: LCSH: Contractors' operations—Vocational guidance—Juvenile literature.
| Construction industry—Juvenile literature. | Contractors—Juvenile literature.
Classification: LCC TA210 .S33 2016 | DDC 690.837—dc23
LC record available at http://lccn.loc.gov/2015034151

Editorial Director: David McNamara
Editors: Andrew Coddington and Kelly Spence
Copy Editor: Rebecca Rohan
Art Director: Jeffrey Talbot
Designer: Alan Sliwinski
Senior Production Manager: Jennifer Ryder-Talbot
Production Editor: Renni Johnson
Photo Research: J8 Media

Printed in the United States of America

Table of Contents

A general contractor and a member of his crew examine the plans for a building they're working on.

Introduction

Imagine if we lived in a world without buildings, roadways, railways, bridges, and most importantly, houses. Where would we live, and how would we get from one place to another? Have you ever looked at your surroundings, and thought about how they were built? Or who had the necessary skills and training to build them? It's easy to take these things for granted, unless perhaps one of your family members or friends works in the construction industry. Everything from buildings and homes, to railroads and bridges, was carefully designed, measured, and built, by skilled people working in construction. When we think of the word "construction," we usually picture a jobsite filled with piles of dirt and yellow, heavy-duty machinery. If you look up the definition of construction in the dictionary, it is defined as "the act or process of building something (such as a house or road)." This definition hardly does construction justice, because "the building of things" comes in so many different shapes and forms.

So, what do we know about construction? Practically everywhere we go these days, there's some sort of construction taking place, whether it's the building of a shopping mall, sidewalk repairs, or roadwork. In a typical year, roughly $1 trillion is spent on construction projects in the United States. An estimated seven million people work in various parts of this industry. The construction field is heavily dominated by male workers, who make up 91 percent of the industry workforce, according to the Occupational Safety and Health Administration (OSHA). One interesting aspect of this field is how vast it is; some small jobs can be accomplished by one person, while others require hundreds of workers to complete. Additionally, there are many different types of construction, such as residential, commercial, and industrial. Within each of these sectors, there are many kinds of construction jobs. Individuals who work in fields like plumbing and electrical are part of the construction workforce. However, where they exactly fit in all depends upon the scope of work involved in a project. But who is responsible for managing a construction site, like a new house or home renovation, and overseeing a project from start to finish? The answer to that question is a general contractor.

A general contractor (GC) is the type of construction worker you would hire to build your house or perform other construction projects around your home. He or she has extensive knowledge of the construction field, hires **subcontractors** to complete a project, and manages the entire project. It's important to establish the core difference between construction and general contracting: construction is the actual work of a general contractor. A general contractor is contracted, or hired, by an individual or organization to construct something—like a house or an office building. General contractor is a specific job title and specialty among the various types of professions within the construction industry. This book will focus on the residential construction career path of a general contractor. Residential construction includes new construction—such as a new housing development—and renovations, which are improvements or upgrades to an existing house. A GC's work is almost always privately commissioned, paid for by the homeowner themselves or a bank. These types of projects are usually designed by **architects** or designers and built by contractors that either run their own company or work as part of a contracting

It is important for a new house to have a strong, stable foundation on which to build the rest of the structure.

firm or agency. Currently, there are more than five hundred thousand contracting companies in the United States.

Throughout the course of this book, you'll learn the ins and outs of the general contracting field. We'll start with the history of the field, learning how the industry has transformed into what it currently is today, while also learning about the qualities that a good GC should have. Next, we'll learn what type of formal education and other training it takes to become a general contractor, as well as other forms of on-the-job training that can be helpful to get started in this field. From there, we'll dig into the many daily responsibilities that a GC holds throughout all phases of a construction project. Lastly, we'll highlight the benefits of a career in general contracting, including areas like annual salary, the rate of growth in the field, health insurance benefits, and the pros and cons of the job. By the end of this book, you'll have a full understanding of the general contracting field and what it takes to become a successful GC.

During Roman times, stone was often used to construct homes, walls, and other buildings.

CHAPTER 1

The Job of a General Contractor

While we can't pinpoint the exact moment that general contracting became a way to earn a living and a recognized profession, we do know that homes have come a long way since the Prehistoric Age, when people lived in caves. That all changed in 43 CE, when the Romans brought construction to Britain and began to use jointing mortar to construct walls as part of their houses. It wasn't until roughly 1200 CE that building regulations were established, with 3-foot (0.9-meter) stone party walls being the standard. During the Elizabethan Age, timber frames were introduced to keep houses sturdy. By the late 1500s, windows started to be added during the building process. During the mid-1850s, builders began to develop townhouses and apartment buildings. This is when contracting began to expand from homes to larger residential projects. The level of skill and craftsmanship used in construction has evolved thanks to an ever-changing array of materials, products, and building techniques. These are responsible for some of the most distinguished buildings and breathtaking structures that have ever been built. Every structure that you see—from the school you attend to the house you live in—was built by a licensed contractor who had the proper education, knowledge, and training to get the job done.

Centuries ago, general contracting was a way of life. It was how people provided shelter for themselves from harsh outdoor conditions. They didn't do it to make money; they did it to survive. That all changed in 1870, at least in the United States, when builders began to accept contracts to construct large buildings across the country. Because most of the building work during this time was commissioned by the government or a public agency, the term "contractor" was used to describe a builder who was contracted by another party to work on a project. Thus, the title "general contractor" was born. It's believed that general contractors became in demand during this time because of the increasing complexity of construction projects and the need for a variety of specialized skills to build or renovate a building. As general contracting began to rise in the United States, two firms in particular influenced the development of the field: the Norcross Brothers and the George A. Fuller Company. The Norcross Brothers were the first wave of general contractors in the country—known for being one of the first general contractors for buildings—and the country's largest by 1900. The George A. Fuller Company was part of the second wave of general contractors. Known for their work on skyscrapers, the George A. Fuller Company was an ingenious group known for its speed and high-quality construction skills. Now that we know the history of general contracting, let's look at what the job entails and what skills are needed in this profession.

Defining a General Contractor

The problem with trying to define who a general contractor is and what he or she does is in its name— it's *general*. A general contractor can wear many hats, but his or her overall job is to act as project manager on a construction project. Also known as a construction manager or an engineer, a GC's main role is to see a project through from start to finish. He or she manages each step of the entire process to ensure quality and safety, both on the jobsite and in the finished product. While a contractor's job is to project-manage, he or she is sometimes also responsible for the labor included in a project—especially in smaller firms, or for contractors who work for themselves. In most cases, general contractors have worked their way up to a management position after spending years honing their skills within a certain specialty, like plumbing, masonry, electrical, or carpentry. Often while an individual is working in a specific trade, they also learn about aspects of the contracting field. This can include how to hire and manage subcontractors, prepare bids and estimate project costs, purchase materials, and create schedules.

The general contracting field is an interesting and fun career path because contractors can choose to either start their own businesses, or work as employees for a contracting company. For those leaning more toward an entrepreneurial path, it's important to note that a lot more work comes with it. Not only are you responsible for delivering the finished product to your clients, but you're also responsible for running a business, and all of the tasks that come along with it. You'll need to decide if you're going to be a one-person shop, or if you want to build a team of subcontractors to work with. Being a one-person shop doesn't necessarily mean that you'll be working by yourself on a project. Contractors who work alone often hire subcontractors to help complete a job.

The benefit to starting a contracting business, which is also sometimes known as a firm or agency, is that you are able to handpick the team that you work with each day on the jobsite. When members of a group become more comfortable with each other, this helps to build trust. That's extremely important because construction sites can be dangerous at times. Either way, whether they're hiring subcontractors or have a regular team of their own, a general contractor is responsible for their employees' work and safety at all times.

The General Contractor's Team

If a GC is working as part of a company or firm, they have a team under them that performs most of the tasks needed to construct a home or building. The contractor's job is to oversee them and make sure that all of the work is being done, properly and on schedule. In this case, a GC's team is typically made up of the following workers:

Project Manager (PM): A project manager is responsible for overseeing that the terms of the contract are met. Typically, the PM is the person who puts the team of workers together—which includes hiring subcontractors—and establishes project milestones and purchase orders.

Subcontractors raise a frame that will become a wall for a house.

Superintendent: A superintendent works in the field alongside his or her team, coordinating the daily production and work activities. The superintendent also serves as the safety officer on the job, making sure that all work gets completed, and that it's being done safely and correctly.

Foreman: A foreman is essentially the manager of the general contractor's workers. A foreman's job is to introduce the work to the team and ensure that the correct tools are available to get the job done. A foreman is also responsible for preparing daily time sheets so that workers' attendance and progress can be tracked.

Field Engineers: Also known as project engineers or assistant superintendents, a field engineer's job is to make sure that information about the project—whether it be roadblocks, a change in timelines, or the need for more materials—gets communicated to the proper person so that the project keeps progressing. A field engineer also maintains project tracking logs and reviews any invoices that are tied to the project.

Subcontractors: Subcontractors are laborers hired by the general contractor to conduct most of the physical work on a project. A subcontractor could be a painter, electrician, plumber, or another construction specialist. Typically, subcontractors specialize in a specific area of the construction field.

As you can see, a general contractor has a large team of individuals who help them to manage the project. On smaller jobs, or when a GC doesn't work as part of a firm or agency (which is sometimes known as self-performing), many of these responsibilities are handled by the contractor and the subcontractors. There are a lot of different qualities that are needed to handle this job, with one of the most important being organization.

The Qualities of a Successful GC

A general contractor must have excellent organization and planning skills to scope out a project and make sure that there are enough workers and materials to get the work done. The GC must also estimate all of the costs for the materials of the project, as part of the role includes purchasing or renting all the materials, tools, and heavy machinery needed to complete the build. Have you ever looked at a house and wondered how many two-by-four

A big part of a GC's job is to update his or her client (the homeowners) on the progress of the project.

pieces of lumber were needed to build it? A contractor can tell you, and should be able to tell you how much they cost, too.

General contractors are also responsible for hiring all the subcontractors who will be working toward the finished product. General contractors have to be knowledgeable about a lot of key areas of construction to fulfill their duties. However, no one can ever know it all, or build an entire house by themselves quickly. This is why a GC needs to hire subcontractors to help. It's up to the general contractor to determine when it's time to bring in the plumber to install the sink and toilet in the bathroom, and when the carpenter should arrive to start building the deck in the backyard Before a project can start, a general contractor must estimate the time and cost needed to obtain the proper **permits**. For most jobs that a general contractor is going to work on, they're going to need a permit from the town or state to begin work. The process of obtaining a permit to start a project varies from state to state. Regardless of where you live, a contractor must go through the proper channels to get a permit. Typically, that process involves a trip to the local town hall or state building, filling out a form, and waiting for approval of the project after it is reviewed by the appropriate officials. In addition to hiring the staff,

The Meaning of a General Contractor

While we know the job title as "general contractor" in the United States, in the United Kingdom and some British Commonwealth countries, a general contractor is known as a "main contractor." People in the UK used to call these workers general contractors, but that term has since been superseded by the more widely-used main contractor. In the UK, the term general contractor is now only used in situations where there's a main contractor, who's the head manager and supervisor of a project, and a general contractor, who works below the main contractor.

purchasing the materials, and securing the permits, a general contractor must also lay out a schedule that establishes goals and deadlines for different phases of construction. It's up to the contractor to make sure the dates for these milestones are realistic and achievable.

General contractors must also have great communication skills. They're responsible for hiring staff and subcontractors to help them complete the project. They're also responsible for managing those employees, and therefore must be able to effectively communicate with them. For example, a contractor may need to speak with an architect or engineer to discuss the layout of the building. Or they may have to talk to an electrician to plan where the electrical box and wiring should go in a house they're building together. No matter who they are speaking to, the general contractor must be able to easily explain and discuss the project's plans and communicate timelines and expectations.

Before any of this can take place, though, the contractor first must win the project from their client. Hiring a contractor isn't an easy decision. Most homeowners will research companies when they're looking for a contractor to build or remodel their home. It's not uncommon for people to conduct interviews with potential contractors prior to hiring them, and to ask questions about their background, crew, process, costs, licenses, and more. GCs must present themselves as qualified professionals and be able to clearly communicate their expertise in building a home. This will give the customer confidence that they're hiring the right person for the job. Once the contractor lands the job, he or she must also be able to discuss the scope of work with the client and help them put their ideas on paper. A good contractor is able to help a client envision what the end product will look like and is able to make the client feel comfortable that the finished build will exceed their expectations. Additionally, it is important for a contractor to keep the client updated on the progress of the build. As potential problems arise, it's important that the contractor be proactive in diagnosing the problem and coming up with a solution, all while keeping the client in the loop. Without great communication skills, a contractor may not be able to manage the project—which is a core responsibility for a general contractor.

A GC must be ready at all times to handle problems and emergencies while also being up-to-date on safety rules and regulations. On a jobsite with dangerous power tools and unsturdy surfaces, a general contractor must make sure the site is safe for their subcontractors and anyone else there. In the event that an accident takes place and an employee is injured, the contractor must be aware of the proper course of action, whether it is applying first aid or calling for an ambulance. Not all emergencies are physically harmful, though; other problems do come up. Let's say that a delivery gets delayed or inclement weather stops the crew from pushing forward with the project— all of those issues fall on the shoulders of the GC. He or she must be ready to make decisions and find new solutions to complete the project on time for the client. Along these same lines, a GC must also be reliable and trustworthy. The homeowner is relying on the contractor

Following proper safety procedures and communication are key to preventing accidents on the jobsite.

to provide quality work and build the home or building to their specifications, all while following building codes and ensuring the work is safe and correct. Additionally, renovation and construction jobs aren't cheap, so a general contractor needs to be trustworthy when it comes to collecting payments from the homeowner and delivering on the finished project. If a GC establishes a reputation as unreliable and dishonest, he or she will not get referrals from many clients.

A good general contractor is a great decision-maker. There is a great deal of responsibility on the shoulders of general contractors, and at the end of the day, it comes down to making smart decisions. Since the general contractor serves as the project manager of a jobsite and supervises an entire project from start to finish, it's crucial that they exercise solid judgment and make smart decisions on the fly. There are many moving parts on a construction site, and the GC must be able to always keep the big picture in mind.

Perhaps the most obvious skill that's missing up to this point is the need to be handy and have the necessary trade skills to complete a job. All contractors should know basic math—or at least how to record proper measurements—as well as how to wield all kinds of tools. It's also important to know about the different types of materials that they're working with, such as what type of wood is best used to withstand the elements. Since the general contractor is in charge of the entire project—think of him or her as a general in the military—it's also their responsibility to check all of the work as it's being done for quality control and to make sure everything is sturdy and built to code.

Hours and Pay

While working as a GC, there are typically no set hours. That could be good or bad, depending on what you're looking for in a job. If you run your own contracting company, you're your own boss, and you're able to decide how many hours you want to work per week. Depending on what's slated for completion from week to week, it's not uncommon for a contractor's schedule and hours to fluctuate. The most important thing, however, is to make sure that the project gets completed on time. That may mean putting in a sixty-hour week toward the end of the project to make sure a deadline is met. That's just what comes along with the territory of being a general contractor. The job must get done. In some cases, the number of hours spent working on the project is how the contractor gets paid. This is called a time and materials contract. With a time and materials contract, a GC bills the client or homeowner by the hour for the amount of time (labor) and the cost of the materials involved in the project. This type of contract is always subject to change throughout the duration of the build, because it's not uncommon for unforeseen issues to come up. The GC will bill for extra hours if this happens.

Another way that a contractor earns money on a home build or remodeling project is by charging a flat fee for the entire project. This is known as a fixed-price contract. This type of contract is more favorable for the homeowner because if unforeseen costs come up, the homeowner isn't liable for paying for them—it essentially gives the GC more motivation to finish the project on time so that they're not paying for additional costs out of their own pocket. Typically, the price of the contract can vary between 10–20 percent of the total cost of the job, including the cost of all subcontractors, materials, permits, and any other costs associated with the project. Additionally, it's not uncommon for a general contractor to charge an upfront down payment of 20–30 percent of the total project cost before work begins.

How Technology is Changing the Game

In the tech-savvy twenty-first century, the fact that GCs and their teams can build a home or building from scratch is truly impressive. Construction is still very much a labor-intensive, manual industry. That's not to say that technology hasn't found its way into the construction and contracting field, though. Technology has benefited GCs by allowing them to start a project faster by using computers to produce 3-D mockups and blueprints for their clients to see before work begins. The technology allows engineers and architects to design building

GCs utilize computers on the job to examine 3-D mockups provided by architects and designers.

Technology on the jobsite provides excellent tools to keep track of schedules, materials, and more.

mockups much faster than if they were to sketch them out on blueprint paper. The use of this technology also helps homeowners approve the design much quicker, and it provides more in-depth plans and instructions for the GC and their team to follow. Once the project is complete, builders are always installing technologies in their clients' homes, such as thermostats, door locks, garage doors, lighting, and more.

Technology has also revolutionized the construction management field. Software programs have been developed that help to forecast estimates for an entire project, which is beneficial when scoping out the price and contract for a job. Once the project begins, contractors and project managers can utilize computer technology to monitor and track their workers' hours and the cost of the project's materials. This software can then be used as a means of communication between team members to streamline projects and assure that all time, materials, and costs are accounted for. Some of the software programs used today include Microsoft Project, Primavera, and Prolog Manager.

General contractors wear many hats and are responsible for everything from reviewing blueprints to managing a team of subcontractors.

CHAPTER 2

What It Takes to Become a General Contractor

In Chapter 1, we learned about all of the qualities needed for a successful career in general contracting. But before you start planning to become a GC, ask yourself if you have an interest in the qualifications necessary to become one. For example, one of the main general interest areas necessary for a contracting career, which may not seem obvious at first, is an interest in and understanding of math. There are a lot of mathematical calculations and formulas that directly translate into the general contracting field. These include the measurement of materials and the calculation of costs associated with a project. Because GCs are responsible for ordering all of the materials associated with a project, they must be able to properly calculate figures and add up costs. Being competent in math is not only helpful, it's a core skill of the job. Having an interest in project management and the confidence to become the lead decision maker will also help you fit well into the general contracting field. GCs are responsible for managing all aspects of a project's build—from the bid and price of the project all the way to the finished product—and supervising others.

Since working in the construction and contracting field is such a hands-on career, those aspiring to be general contractors should like working with their hands, in addition to being interested in how things are built. While general contractors may not do much of the work themselves on a jobsite, this is because they've spent countless hours working their way up to this management position. Working outdoors is another benefit (in good weather!) of this profession. If a GC is put in charge of the construction of a new home, they're going to be working outside for a good portion of the project, as the foundation gets laid and the frame of the house is built. Some jobs can become boring because you're doing the same thing every day, but that's definitely not the case when you're a general contractor. Once a project is complete, you can move onto something new and challenging. All of these interests, combined with an education and/or experience in the construction field can lead to a successful career as a GC.

While general contractors are largely responsible for managing subcontractors, at times they must roll up their sleeves and take part in the actual construction of the project.

The general contracting field has come a long way from the Prehistoric Age, and the driving force behind that is the education available today to aspiring GCs. Today, students are able to take advantage of more integrated technology and resources that allow them to excel and receive a hands-on learning experience. From an outsider's perspective, it may look like an easy job, but there's a ton of education and training needed to become a licensed contractor. While it varies from state to state, a license is typically required before a contractor is able to start working. The type and cost of the project ultimately determines whether a contractor needs to have a license

It's never too early to start learning the skills necessary for a career as a general contractor. High school classes in mathematics and business management are a great start.

to accept a job. In some states, any job that costs more than a few hundred dollars requires a license, while other states have a threshold in the thousands of dollars range. It's well-known in the industry that commercial projects usually have different—and more substantial— requirements than residential projects. There are a few different educational paths that a person can take to become a professional general contractor, with each providing different benefits and experiences.

High School

If you are interested in pursuing a career as a GC, you can start building your skills in high school. Courses in English, mathematics, and business management are beneficial to working in this field. Any construction-specific classes or clubs, such as woodworking, welding, and drafting, are also useful. You can also volunteer for projects like Habitat for Humanity to gain real-world experience on a jobsite. It's never too early to start preparing and learning more about the growing field of construction.

Post-Secondary Education

While it's not a requirement, it is preferred by larger firms that their general contractors have a bachelor's degree. Additionally, according to the US Bureau of Labor

Statistics (BLS), GCs with a college degree typically get hired ahead of those without one. Like any college degree, a BA looks great on a résumé and shows companies and clients that you're well-educated and take your career seriously. According to www.LearnHowToBecome. org, there are more than one hundred institutions in the United States that offer degrees in fields like construction science, building science, and construction engineering—all degree areas that can lead to a career in general contracting. It's important to note that in the event that an aspiring contractor only wants to work on small projects, an associate's degree may be sufficient. However, to advance in a GC career and earn a higher salary, it's best to acquire a bachelor's degree, and in some cases, even earn a master's degree in a specialized field. The benefit of obtaining a formal education and college degree in the general contracting field is learning about all aspects of the discipline. You're able to study it, a few sections at a time, to understand the entire process from a large-scale perspective. Of course, each institution will have its own specific classes that make up its curriculum. For example, below are seven required courses that make up part of the New York University School of Professional Studies' Construction Project Management degree program:

Reading and Interpreting Construction Drawings:
Since it's a necessity for project managers to be able to read construction plans, this course covers plans and drawings for reinforced concrete, steel, wood frame, and masonry construction in addition to mechanical and electrical construction. Floor plans, elevations, symbols, schedules, and architectural abbreviations are also taught.

Principles of Project Management: This course teaches the essentials of project management on a construction site, including the stages of design, planning, implementation, and evaluation. These skills all tie into effective cost and time management. The course also covers project organization and team selection, establishing objectives, determining project timelines and milestones, how to allocate resources, and ultimately measuring the performance, status, and reporting on an entire project.

Construction Project Management: The construction project management course gives students an overview of the construction industry and its processes, and teaches them how to properly and effectively manage projects. Students will learn the roles of owners, architects, engineers, and contractors, as well as team organization, the bidding and awarding process of a project, budgets, cost estimation, construction planning and scheduling, accounting systems, claims and disputes, safety and insurance, bonds, and liens.

Construction Law: The construction law course sheds light on the legal issues that can occur during the construction process, including bidding and contract layout, contract conditions, subcontracts, architects and engineers, privity of contracts, defaults and termination, the changing of conditions, extra work, lien law, **surety bonds**, fraud, mistakes, delays, and how to dispute and resolve issues.

Construction Project Scheduling and Control: This is an in-depth course that highlights the critical path method (CPM) and additional analytical and quantitative scheduling and management approaches. This course uses Microsoft Project specifically, in addition to case studies, problems, and exercises. Topics include feasibility studies, project planning, network development, resource costs and allocation, schedule and budget control programs, and time and cost analysis.

Construction Cost Estimating: The main purpose of this class is to teach students how to develop project estimates and the final bid price for a project. Topics covered include the bidding process as a whole, the bid package, general conditions of a bid, subcontractor bid comparisons, planning of an estimate, management considerations, conceptualization, preliminary budgets, review of a design, detailed estimates, unit prices, lump-sum bids, costs, overhead, bonds, and insurance.

Construction Financial and Cost Management: This course is designed to teach the concepts of project and program cost management. Students learn cost estimating and scheduling, how to properly allocate costs, direct and indirect costs, overhead, risk and contingency, dispute resolution, financial evaluation techniques and earned value analysis, including multiple payment terms like cost-to-complete, percent complete, cost at completion, and other **preconstruction** services for budget management.

As you can see from the course descriptions, following a traditional educational path can be informative and beneficial. You may have noticed that some of the courses overlap, which is standard for many college programs. The overlapping of subject areas helps to keep students up-to-date—especially in the event that a law or code changes—and it also helps students to retain information. If you were to only learn new information in one course, there's a good chance that you may not remember and retain that information as much as you would if it was being repeated and taught in new ways in different classes. Sometimes an associate's degree paired with years of hands-on experience can be substituted for a bachelor's degree, but that's often on a case-by-case basis. All in all, it may be beneficial for you to study construction management, or a similar program, to hone your craft and prepare you for the general contracting field.

On-the-Job Training

It doesn't matter what industry you're in, whether it's in digital marketing or construction—hands-on training is often the best way to learn a skill. This is especially true for general contractors. On-the-job training is a common and effective route to becoming a GC. Also, if you don't plan to pursue a post-secondary education, as a young professional you may be hired as an assistant under a general contractor—either as a plumber, mason, electrician, carpenter, or other construction specialty. This person will show you the ropes of the job. As you work daily alongside the experienced GC, you'll gradually learn all of the different skills necessary to become a general contractor and can eventually apply for a license in your particular trade. This type of on-the-job training can range from less than a year to several years, depending on how quickly you pick up on the daily responsibilities of the

Apprenticeships provide on-the-job training and are one of the best ways to get your foot in the door as a GC.

job, as well as how many different areas of contracting you want to specialize in.

Another form of on-the-job training is an **apprenticeship**, which can be offered through a construction company, trade association, or trade union for aspiring general contractors. An apprenticeship is beneficial because you receive both on-the-job and formal classroom training. There are usually a designated number of hours that an apprentice must complete in the field and in the classroom. For instance, the

San Diego Associate General Contractors Apprenticeship Program states that apprentices must attend two night classes per week for a minimum of twenty-four weeks in a calendar year to meet the requirements of the apprenticeship. Their trade options include carpenters, cement masons, drywall finishers, drywall lathers, heavy equipment operators, laborers, and painters. This particular apprenticeship has a minimum age requirement of eighteen, and candidates must have proof of a high school diploma or GED, plus the ability to work in the United States. An additional benefit of an apprenticeship is that apprentices collect a salary throughout their apprenticeship. Not only are they receiving on-the-job training and gaining knowledge in the classroom, they're also getting paid to work toward their career—that's not something that a lot of college students can say. And while an apprenticeship typically takes anywhere from two to five years, upon its completion, general contractors receive a certificate and are fully employed, which can really jumpstart their careers.

Meeting Licensing Requirements and Obtaining Surety Bonds

Regardless of which route you take—whether it's a traditional college education or an apprenticeship through an accredited union or company—in order to become a

Online Opportunities for GCs

An apprenticeship doesn't necessarily have to be completed inside a traditional classroom. For example, the Independent Electrical Contractors Rocky Mountain (IECRM) association offers an online apprenticeship called the Live-Online Program. This online program serves as an alternative to classroom sessions and has benefited hundreds of students. The IECRM launched the online program in 2009, the first in the country, which is recognized by the US Department of Labor (DOL) Office of Apprenticeship (OA/BAT) and also approved and regulated by the Colorado Department of Higher Education, Division of Private Occupational Schools Board. The IECRM represents more than two hundred member companies who are responsible for more than $2 billion of construction per year. The IECRM educates more than one thousand electrical apprentices and licensed electricians every year. Their online apprenticeship program is beneficial for individuals who either have families that they need to take care of at home, or for young individuals who are working more than one job. Overall, the IECRM's online program continues to show how technological advancements create new opportunities within the contracting and construction field.

licensed contractor, you must pass an exam. This exam varies depending on which state a GC wants to be licensed in. If you want to be able to work on jobs like residential homes, corporate office buildings, roadways, retail stores and plazas, government buildings, bridges, and other structures, you will also need to pass a state exam before a license is issued. In addition to passing the exam, there are a few other requirements necessary to become a licensed general contractor. An individual must be at least eighteen years of age, possess a high

Applying for a license isn't always the easiest process but it is beneficial for general contractors looking to work on higher-paying jobs.

school diploma or GED, be able to legally work in the United States, and have a clean working record in the construction field without any incidents. Additionally, certain states also require that contractors have proof of liability insurance and a business address, and show a federal Tax Identification Number. Another necessity for obtaining a license is having practical experience in the construction field—this is where on-the-job training and apprenticeships come in handy. If you received a college education in construction management or a related field, you'll likely already have the hands-on experience needed to pass the exam and obtain a contractor's license.

The benefit of becoming a licensed contractor is that you will be viewed as trustworthy and knowledgeable in the construction field, thus giving you an advantage over unlicensed contractors. Licensed contractors typically charge more for their work than those that are unlicensed, because unlicensed contractors don't have to pay for licensing charges or liability/worker's compensation insurance. Contractor's licenses are partially in place to protect the welfare and health of the public for whom the contractor is working. Failing to have a license when working on a job that requires one can be damaging to a GC's career and well-being, as there can be serious financial and disciplinary ramifications for violating the rules. Being a licensed contractor helps to establish credibility on the job, which ultimately justifies being able to charge upfront deposits and higher rates for projects. It's important to note that there is a limit to the amount that a GC can charge as a deposit. For example, in California, general contractors are limited to charging 10 percent of the total job or $1,000, whichever is the smaller figure. People are usually willing to pay more if they know that a licensed professional is managing the project and quality can be assured. Additionally, large businesses and corporations generally only hire contractors who are licensed professionals, and many homeowner policies also require that any work done to a home is completed by a licensed building contractor.

In many states, it's also required that a contractor is "bonded" in order to obtain a license; the official term is called a contractor's license bond. What this does is assure the client that the GC is operating within the proper laws and regulations of the industry. These construction bonds are available for purchase through a **surety,** or a company that sells construction bonds to contractors. This type of bond also protects the client if the contractor is unable to complete the job properly or fails to pay for permits, subcontractors, or any other financial responsibilities. Like many aspects of the general contracting field, the need for a contractor being bonded depends on which state he or she is working in. For example, in California, the Contractor's State License Board requires that contractors obtain a license bond when they are first awarded their contractor's license. The bond costs a GC roughly $100, and it can pay a GC's client up to $12,500 to cover faulty work or other various license law infractions. Additionally, there are a few specific types of bonds that address different types of risks that a contractor may be required to purchase. Each unique bond benefits the client and has to be purchased separately by the GC. Let's take a look at those bonds and find out their purposes.

Bid Bond: The purpose of a **bid bond** is to assure that a client doesn't pay more for a project than what was agreed upon by the winning contractor. This is beneficial to a homeowner in the event that the winning bidder backs out of the project and a second contractor submitted a higher bid. A bid bond is usually issued for 5 to 10 percent of the total dollar value of the bid. For example, let's say Contractor One submits a bid for $1,000,000 and includes a bid bond worth $100,000 (10 percent of the bid). The next lowest bidder, Contractor Two, submits a bid of $1,060,000. The homeowner chooses Contractor One because it's the cheapest bid, but Contractor One receives a higher-paying job and decides not to sign the contract. Now, that homeowner has to spend $60,000 more than they originally thought, because they're forced to sign with Contractor Two. Because of the bid bond, the surety is responsible for paying the owner up to the maximum value of the bid bond, which in this case, was $100,000. The homeowner will then get the difference between the two bids—$60,000—in addition to any related costs, up to $100,000 (the value of the bid bond). From there, the surety will seek reimbursement from Contractor One.

Performance Bond: A **performance bond** assures a homeowner that the scope of work that was agreed upon at the price of the bid will be completed. In the event that a general contractor defaults on the project, the surety typically covers 100 percent of the bid amount to assure that the project gets done for the homeowner. There are a few different ways that the surety can handle a default by a contractor. They can finance the original contractor or provide him or her with the necessary support to get the job done, or they can hire a replacement contractor to come in and complete the work. The surety can also pay the homeowner the financial amount necessary to complete the work, up to the total bid amount.

Payment Bond: Payment bonds were created to assure homeowners that any subcontractors or **suppliers** that assisted in a project will get paid by the general contractor. Payment bonds are usually issued in conjunction with performance bonds. As we've learned so far, subcontractors and suppliers play essential roles for general contractors and are essential in the completion of a project. While it's the responsibility of the GC to pay the subcontractors and suppliers, if he or she doesn't, the subcontractors and suppliers can take legal action against the homeowner, which is why payment bonds are so important. Like performance bonds, payment bonds are typically issued for 100 percent of the contract price and are administered when the contract is finalized and signed.

It's clear to see that these bonds are in place to protect a homeowner from unsatisfactory work by a general contractor and his or her team, which is something that unfortunately becomes an issue sometimes in the contracting and construction field. There are individuals who may seem like they have all of the necessary training and skills to complete a job, but sometimes the end result doesn't reflect what the general contractor has promised to the client. This is why homeowners are advised to do a lot of research before hiring a contractor to work on their house.

For a general contractor to work, he or she needs to purchase a surety bond from a surety company.

Now that we know the different types of contractor's bonds and why they're so important to a homeowner, it's time to learn how a GC qualifies to buy a surety bond. While each surety company has its own criteria in determining if a general contractor meets the requirements to purchase a surety bond, the three main areas that will be the deciding factor are the contractor's **capacity, capital**, and **character**. To determine the three Cs, a surety will have a contractor fill out a form that asks various questions related to current and past work, financial values tied to current and past projects, types of jobs completed in the past, bank statements, references, and more. Here's what the three different Cs mean:

Capacity: This is the contractor's qualification and skill set to be able to understand the scope of work and complete a project from start to finish. A general contractor's years of experience, past work history, current projects being worked on, and organization and management are all factored into the determination of their capacity. Think of it as the general contractor's ability to take on a new job at that current time.

Capital: This is the amount of money that the general contractor has, which also translates into his or her ability to finance a project, which includes being able to pay for subcontractors and suppliers. The surety will also want to be confident that the contractor has enough capital to cover any unforeseen financial troubles that arise during a project. The general contractor's bank records and other financial assets will be reviewed during this process.

Character: This refers to the integrity of the general contractor or company he or she is employed by. A surety will typically use resources like the Better Business Bureau to check past work history and to see if there have been any complaints filed against the contractor or the company. If so, that would signal a breach of character and decrease the chances of the GC receiving the bond. It's also not uncommon for testimonials from former clients to be utilized when determining the character of a general contractor.

Certifications

Though it's not required, a contractor may want to pursue a certification or specific credential to specialize in a certain area or to qualify for a particular job. An example of this would be if a general contractor wanted to obtain a certification in asbestos removal for a restoration job. This is an extra type of certification that makes GCs more versatile in their everyday work and can help lead to more advanced work and higher-paying jobs. One way for a general contractor to advance his or her career is by becoming a Certified Construction Manager (CCM) through the Construction Management Association of America (CMAA). Established in 1982, the CMAA is North America's only organization that's dedicated to professional construction and program management. The association is made up of more than fourteen thousand individuals and has twenty-eight regional and fifty student chapters at colleges and institutions around the United States. Additionally, contractors can

General contractors who receive additional certificates are eligible for more advanced work and higher-paying jobs.

obtain further certifications through other organizations like the American Institute of Contractors (AIC), an institution dedicated to providing the means for obtaining credentials within the contracting and construction fields. To be eligible for the CCM certification through the CMAA, a contractor must have a minimum of forty-eight months' experience as a construction manager. Other eligibilities for the certification program include a bachelor's degree in construction management, construction science, engineering, or architecture; an associate's degree combined with four years of experience in construction; or a high school diploma or GED combined with eight years of construction experience. The certification exam lasts five hours and tests contractors in the areas of project management, cost management, and time management.

Overall, you can see that there's a lot of education, training, and work that goes into becoming a general contractor. From educational courses and hands-on training to licensing and certification exams, becoming a professional, licensed, general contractor isn't a walk in the park, but it can be a rewarding career. Think about it. You're building homes from scratch and giving clients a place to call home. For higher-end clients, you may be building them their dream home, complete with all of the features and functionality that they've been wanting for years. Given the amount of work that's put into designing and building a home or building, contractors are paid very well for their services (this will be discussed in more detail in Chapter 4). The bottom line is that becoming a GC is a rewarding career, and one that is self-fulfilling. One of the most beneficial aspects of being a general contractor is that you are always learning new things. You always have the opportunity to set new personal goals and take your career to the next level, and obtain new certifications to advance your knowledge and job opportunities in the construction industry.

It's important that general contractors communicate to their subcontractors what needs to be done on a jobsite.

CHAPTER 3

The Day-to-Day Responsibilities of a General Contractor

What are some of the most common duties and responsibilities a general contractor encounters on a day-to-day basis? What are the three main phases of construction, and what role does the general contractor play in each? Before we can dive into the answers to these questions, you need to remember: a general contractor can't start anything until he or she has landed the job.

Bidding on a Job

In order to get a new construction job, a general contractor must prepare a bid, or quote, to take on the project. A lot of time and effort goes into preparing a construction bid. Before even getting to the point of preparing the bid, the GC must decide if it's even worth taking time away from his or her current workload to prepare a bid for a new job. A general contractor must also consider the current workload of the contractor or firm representing him or her; the type, size, and location of the project; the availability of subcontractors and other workers as well as suppliers; the amount of competition also bidding on the same job; and the amount of funding that the owner has to allocate to the project and to the GC and his team to do the construction, to name a few. Additionally, as part of the bid preparation, a GC tries to estimate the costs needed to complete the project. A GC needs to make sure that they're accurate with their estimations—one wrong calculation or projection can mean a financial loss on a job. The two biggest things that a general contractor needs to budget for are subcontractors and suppliers. General contractors need to pay the subcontractors who are performing the labor for the project, and they also need to pay suppliers for all of the materials and tools—things like lumber, concrete, doors, windows, stone, machines, and power tools—that are needed to complete the build. The estimation of these costs, which also must include the general contractor's fees and pay, become part of the bid that's submitted to the client. It's only once a bid is accepted and the client agrees to work with the GC that any type of project planning or construction can begin.

Preconstruction

Once a general contractor gets chosen by the client, the real work begins. The general contractor plays a crucial role and assumes the bulk of the responsibility on a new building project. In conjunction with having to oversee the entire project and make sure that the project gets completed, the GC has to take part in the preconstruction phase. Preconstruction refers to the actions and set up that are needed in order for construction to start. It's during this phase that permits are obtained, the architect's blueprints and plans are approved by the client, timelines are established, the construction team of subcontractors and other employees are hired and assigned their job roles, **mobilization** takes place, and materials are purchased. Below you'll see how the general contractor plays an intricate role in all aspects of the preconstruction stage.

Conduct a Preconstruction Review: Prior to any work starting, the GC must complete a preconstruction review. This includes reviewing the design to determine if it's possible to build within the budget allotted for the project. During this task, the general contractor is putting a lot of different things in motion for the project, including planning out the jobsite and where everything is going to go, and setting up payroll for the subcontractors.

General contractors play a crucial role in preconstruction, examining the design for the job and analyzing the jobsite.

The preconstruction review also ties in with the next responsibility, which is interacting with the architect or design team.

Interact with the Architect or Design Team: Before any of the work begins, the general contractor will review the plans with the architect to look over the design again, make sure that they have all of the necessary materials, and assure that they match with the scope of work and the timeline in which it needs to be completed. It's crucial that this type of meeting takes place if an architect is involved, as it's important that any problems or issues get resolved before construction begins. Architects aren't always involved in building projects, but since the GC's job is to build and not design, it's often recommended that an architect or designer be hired to conceptualize the design and use their expertise to help bring a project to life for the client. Even once the general contractor's team starts the construction stage, the GC and architect continue to meet and make sure that the construction is following the design plans laid out from the beginning.

Establish Timelines: Establishing timelines for a build is one of the most important yet difficult aspects of a general contractor's duties. The reason it's such a difficult part of the job is because it's so easy and quite common for timelines to change throughout the project. At the onset, the general contractor is tasked with laying out a timeline of milestones that fit the feasibility of everyone working on the project, from subcontractors to suppliers. A GC must try and make an educated guess when scoping out the project as to when certain parts of the project will begin. Some of those parts include when the foundation will be poured; when the structure will begin to be built; when the roof will be built and added to the building; when to call in the plumber so that all pipes, sinks, and toilets can be installed; when the electrician should come in to run all of the wiring and install the electric boxes; and many more. An experienced general contractor will be able to plan out the amount of time that a project is going to take, but one of the hardest parts about planning a timeline is that there's always one known variable: the weather. Inclement weather conditions, such as freezing temperatures, rain, and snow can bring a sudden halt to a project. This in turn throws a wrench into the entire timeline of completion. For example, bad weather can prevent the foundation from being poured, which in turn can delay the walls from going up. Then the plumbers and electricians can't start on time, and perhaps now this job overlaps with another that the plumber had previously committed to, and now he or she is unavailable to work

0								2012					DRAFT				MT
N	N	N	N	D	D	D	D	J	J	J	J	J	F	F	F	F	M	M	M	M
7	14	21	28	5	12	19	26	2	9	16	23	30	6	13	20	27	5	12	19	2
2	3	4	5	6	7	8	9	10	11	12	13	14	15	16	17	18	19	20	21	2

START

REVIEW VENDOR

PROPOSED SCHED

KICK-OFF MEETING

11/25/2014 P

RevA PROCUREMENT

F

PROPOSED SCHEDULE

Establishing and meeting deadlines is the lifeblood of a general contractor's job and success in the field.

on this project. There are also other unexpected setbacks that can arise. For example, a supplier might have an unexpected issue of their own and be unable to get the supplies and materials to the construction team on time, or a subcontractor might become ill or get hurt on the job. These are all obstacles that a GC must deal with. That's why a good GC will build some extra time into the schedule to account for any unexpected delays due to weather or other unforeseen stoppages, so the GC and his or her team can still deliver the finished project to the client on time.

Secure Permits: As we've discussed already, most projects that a general contractor takes on will require a permit to begin work. In most cases, a construction, building, or zoning permit is required before any new build can start. These types of permits are not only required by the local government, but they're also in place to show that the construction being done won't hurt the environment or have any negative effect on the local community. It's the general contractor's job to do all of the legwork to obtain the permit, which usually involves filling out paperwork at town hall, paying for the permit, and then waiting for approval. Prior to even attempting to obtain a permit, it's the GC's job to research the local laws of the area to see what types of permits and licenses are required to start construction. As you already know, the laws and regulations differ by location, so the GC must do his or her due diligence to find out this information before moving forward.

Hire and Manage Subcontractors: General contractors hire subcontractors—also known as subs—to work on the project. The GC must then manage the subcontractors and make sure that the work is completed. For small projects, it's not uncommon for the GC to work with a small crew of only a few workers to complete an entire project—from the pouring of the foundation to the building of the frame, all the way to installing the electrical system. For the everyday project, though, general contractors hire subcontractors who specialize in certain areas of construction to help them get the job done. When looking to hire a subcontractor, a GC will often consult with other subcontractors. Since they all work in the industry together, there's a good chance that your subcontractors know other subs who are looking for work. In some cases, subcontractors (known as **first-tier subcontractors**) even hire other subcontractors (**second-tier subcontractors**) to work under them to help complete a project. The hiring process of a subcontractor can vary based on how the GC goes about it. In some cases, the general contractor has a well-known network of subs that he or she uses on a regular basis. In other cases, subcontractors will submit bids to the GC to work on the project, and the general contractor then has to sort through those bids to assemble his or her team for the project. Once the subs are hired, the management of them takes up a lot of the general contractor's time. It's in the GC's best interest to hire subs who he or she knows are trustworthy; that way they don't need to micromanage them and will not run into any issues with them not showing up for work when they're scheduled. If issues do arise, since the general contractor is in charge of the jobsite, it's his or her responsibility to discipline or fire subcontractors who do not meet the expectations and quality that the GC promised to the client.

Mobilization: Once the client approves the project and the preconstruction review has been conducted, mobilization onto the site can begin. Mobilization means that the general contractor and his crew can set up an office—typically in a mobile trailer—that's kept on the

Construction trailers are a home away from home for GCs and their crew during a job.

jobsite. Part of this responsibility includes laying out a plan of the jobsite and where everything will go. Planning for things like where the office will go and how trucks and pedestrians will access the jobsite, in addition to putting up a fence around the perimeter of the site, is important to streamline the process of preconstruction and mobilization. Also during this process, temporary water and power are set up for the crew, and tools, machinery, and equipment are also brought to the site so that construction can begin. Although the setup process of mobilization takes place at the onset of the project, the trailer that's moved onto the jobsite essentially serves as the office for the GC throughout the duration of the build.

Purchase Materials: The cost of the materials needed for the project may have already been estimated and scoped out, but the general contractor still needs to contact his or her supplier and actually purchase them. It's in the general contractor's best interest to work with a lumberyard or supplier that will guarantee their prices and allow the contractor to open a contractor's account, which allows them to pay for the cost of the materials monthly instead of having to come up with the cash up front. Once the payment structure is settled, a bulk order is usually placed at the beginning of the project. It's not uncommon for the

GC to be in ongoing contact with the supplier to purchase more materials as the need for them arises throughout construction. Once you are established in your career as a GC, you will usually have a regular supplier (or a few) that you always order your materials from.

Breaking Ground

The construction phase is when the building and labor of the project actually takes place. It's during this time that jobs such as pouring the foundation and constructing the walls are completed, as well as interior and exterior painting, building the roof, renovating the bathrooms, and potentially even landscaping. As far as the general contractor goes, it's during the construction phase that he or she acts mostly as the supervisor and project manager of the entire construction project. On smaller jobs, it's not uncommon for the GC to do a lot of the labor-intensive work themselves, but for the most part, that's left to the subcontractors, and it's the general contractor's job to supervise all aspects of the project. Here are some of the duties of a general contractor during the construction phase.

Communicate with Client: We already know that having great communication skills is an absolute necessity for being a general contractor. The main reason behind that is

Finding and maintaining a good working relationship with a reliable supplier can be extremely beneficial for a GC.

because the GC needs to provide progress updates to their clients. For larger projects and new builds, homeowners can't live in their homes while the construction is being done, so they must live elsewhere for that time period and are understandably anxious to get back into their homes as soon as possible. Quite often, homeowners will request weekly—sometimes even daily—status updates from the general contractor. If an unexpected delay comes up and changes need to be made to the timeline, it's important that the GC alerts his or her client and provides solid reasoning as to why. It's also crucial for the GC to be able to explain what's happening in detail for their clients. Most clients aren't construction experts—that's why they hired a GC—so they may not be familiar with the terminology that's used by the contractor and construction team. The GC needs to be able to provide a clear explanation as to what's being done. Lastly, if it's the first time that a client is working with a general contractor, or with one in particular, there's still a trust factor that needs to be established, which makes communication all the more important.

Manage and Oversee Subcontractors: The day-to-day management of a GC's subs is arguably the single most important responsibility of a general contractor once actual construction begins. Because the actual construction of the home or building is the main driver behind getting a project completed on time, a GC must be on top of his team to make sure that they're working diligently while also building a quality structure. Sometimes, if subcontractors don't feel they're being paid what they're worth, they may not work as hard as a GC wants them to. It's important that the general contractor stays in constant contact with his team and gets the best

A Contractor's Punch List

Throughout a project like building a brand-new house, certain areas of the project may not get completed exactly when the timeline had originally stated. Because of that, general contractors have something called a punch list. This serves as a running list for GCs to track adjustments and repairs as they go. These are items that will still need to be completed before the final payment from the client is handed over. Failure to include items on the punch list can seriously delay payment for a GC. According to the American Institute of Architects (AIA) General Conditions, "Failure to include an item on such a list does not alter the responsibility of the contractor to complete all work in accordance with the contract documents." What that means is that the general contractor is responsible for any faulty or incomplete work that the client finds after the closeout period. It's important to know that punch list items don't affect the client from moving into their home. Some examples of what might be included on a general contractor's punch list include sweeping away dust and dirt from the walkway or cleaning tile grout in the shower. Only after all punch list items have been completed can the architect conduct a pre-final inspection, then issue the certificate of substantial completion, which then allows the homeowner to release payment to the general contractor.

work out of them. It's not uncommon for GCs to review the project with his or her subcontractors at the end of each day to make sure that the work is being done properly and that they're still on pace to finish the project within the slated timeline. If the general contractor feels that his or her subs aren't delivering the type of quality that's needed for the project, it's their job to be proactive and notify the sub or potentially let them go.

Post-Construction

By the end of the project—once the structure has been built—everyone is ready to be finished with the project and wrap up the jobsite. They've spent countless hours on the job and are ready to move onto the next site to start a new project. Even once the building has been completed, the general contractor's job isn't finished. The project has now entered the post-construction phase, or construction closeout, where there are numerous tasks that still need to be completed by the GC. These are the tasks that the GC must complete once the project is finished.

Administer Payments: The GC is responsible for hiring subcontractors and suppliers, but he or she is also liable for administering payment to them. It's important that the GC pays his or her subcontractors and suppliers on time to maintain a good working relationship and abide by solid business ethics. As discussed in Chapter 2, subcontractors and suppliers can take legal action against a homeowner if they're not paid. They can also file a lawsuit against the general contractor or the firm he or she is represented by if they don't receive their pay in a timely manner. If the GC likes the work done by the subs or the materials purchased from the supplier, it only makes sense for him or her to make sure that they're paid on time and at the rate that was agreed upon. At the end of a project, the subs are responsible for submitting their

It's the general contractor's responsibility to make sure that subcontractors are paid fairly and on time.

final payment requests, and the GC is then responsible for paying the subcontractors.

Coordinate Inspections: When a structure like a home or building is constructed, it's obviously important that it was built safely and to code, which is why all projects require the proper inspection, usually from outside agencies. Those agencies are usually known as **authorities having jurisdiction (AHJ)**. Their job is to ensure that every project complies with health, safety, and public welfare regulations. If they find that it does, they will then issue a **certificate of occupancy**, which gives the homeowners the right to move into their new home (or move back into their old one). Another form of inspection is completed by the architect. Once the architect is satisfied, he or she will issue a certificate of substantial completion, which states that the home or building can be used for its intended purpose. Additionally, home inspectors are usually brought onto a jobsite in the case of a new-home build or remodeling project to assure that the home is safe, once all of the construction tasks have been completed. Inspectors are also involved at the beginning, before construction even starts, to inspect the premises and make sure that it's clear for the job to begin.

Demobilization: Once the project has been completed, the general contractor packs up his or her jobsite and moves the trailer off the client's property and onto the next jobsite, which is known as **demobilization**. It's the GC's responsibility to make sure that all waste is cleaned up afterward, any security fences or other structures are removed, and that he or she notifies the power company to disconnect the power that was hooked up to their trailer or office. After completely removing the trailer from the site, it's best practice for the GC to do another walkthrough of the jobsite to make sure that there wasn't anything left behind, and that they leave the property clean. Homeowners will be irritated and dissatisfied if a contractor or worker leaves a home it dirtier than it was when they first arrived.

Contractor Closeout: A crucial part of the post-construction phase is the contractor's closeout with his or her team. This involves the GC doing an audit and evaluation of how the entire project went, from start to finish. The GC will discuss the performance of his or her subcontractors with the team and document the team's notes so that they can use what they've learned from this project for the next one. As technology has continued to evolve in construction, a lot of GCs are now using online tools and software to store their job notes, so that they can easily access and reference them for the next job. The closeout will also be the measurement of the success of the project. Documenting if the client's expectations were met, if the client was happy with the general contractor's work, and if the GC and his team met their own profit goal, are all noted at this time.

Submit the Application for Final Payment: After the punch list has been completed, the jobsite has been cleared, and the inspections have been conducted by the architect and AHJ, or another home inspector or outside agency, the general contractor can submit the application for final payment from the client. Although the GC has been getting paid on a monthly basis and may have also received an upfront deposit, there's still a final payment that he or she receives that makes all of the work worth it.

Overall, you can see the many tasks that a general contractor must tend to throughout the course of a project, in addition to sometimes even doing the work themselves, and not counting the endless questions and dialogue that the GC has with his or her team and client throughout the build. Throughout each aspect of the project, from the preconstruction review, to the mobilization, to the construction and the contractor closeout, it's easy to see that a general contractor must be diligent and communicative in every role associated with the job. There are a lot of moving parts on a jobsite, and if a GC doesn't do a great job of keeping the site and his or her team organized, it can lead to a lot of problems and missed deadlines. At the end of the day, there's a lot of work involved with being a general contractor, but it's a rewarding career.

It's a great feeling for a GC to be able to shake their clients' hands and congratulate them on their new home.

CHAPTER 4

Job Outlook and Benefits of the General Contracting Field

You may feel like you're ready to start a long, rewarding career as a general contractor. Before making a final decision, though, it's important to do your research and learn about the field and position you're interested in. Whether your interest lies in general contracting or not, there are questions you need to find out the answers to before committing to any career. You should be asking questions like, "Am I entering a growing field?" "What's the hiring rate for this field?" "Will I have benefits and health insurance for myself and potential family?" Salary, of course, is usually on the minds of most people when doing job research, but health benefits and career growth potential are just as important.

How Much Does a General Contractor Make?

To this point, we've learned that general contractors can get paid various ways, from fixed-price contracts to those that are based on time and materials. Like many aspects of a GC's position, salaries vary based on job type and location. According to the BLS, the average construction manager made $93,900 per year in 2011. That's quite an impressive income, especially when you consider that the average worker across all industries earned $34,750 in 2012—that's $59,150 more that a GC made the prior year than the average worker one year later. Right now, you're probably realizing that all of the school, training, and hard work is worth it to earn that type of salary, and that 2011's near-$94,000 mark was only the average for the year. The same 2011 data stated that the top 10 percent of highest-paid general contractors made $71.67 per hour, which equates to an impressive $149,070 per year. The 10 percent of lowest-paid contractors earned less than $24.34 per hour, or $50,650 annually. While that's a big difference—$98,420 to be exact—between the top and bottom 10-percenters, the $50,650 salary for GCs most likely reflects those who are new to the field.

When looking at more recent data, from May 2014, the BLS's data shows that construction managers/

general contractors in the 10th percentile earned $340 more dollars than they did in 2011, coming in at $50,990 annually. The top 10 percent, or those in the 90th percentile, also saw an increase of $1,180 in that three-year span, making $150,250 per year. For those interested in the residential construction field, individuals in that field earned an average salary of $86,270 in 2014, which works out to $41.48 per hour. It's well known throughout the construction industry that nonresidential jobs, which are sometimes known as commercial construction jobs, are more often profitable for a general contractor. Those working in the nonresidential building construction field in 2014 earned $46.26 per hour, or $96,220 annually. The highest average annual salary of all construction management positions reported by the BLS for 2014 went to individuals in the utility system construction field, where the average worker took home $97,220 per year. Utility system construction workers are responsible for construction on water and sewer lines, oil and gas pipelines, and/or power and communication lines. Overall, the increase in hourly wages and annual salary from 2011 to 2014 for general contractors and construction managers shows that it's a valuable career to get into and one with tremendous growth potential.

The general contracting field can be profitable, which allows GCs to provide well for themselves and their families.

Health Benefits and Insurance

In this line of work, where injury is more common than in other fields, it's important that a general contractor has health insurance. GCs who are employed by a firm are likely covered, but those that have their own company or work on their own do not have guaranteed health benefits. As an independent contractor, or a general contractor who owns his or her own business and works for themselves, it's up to them to obtain health insurance for themselves and their families, which can be a daunting task. The constant changes to the coverage and benefits, paired with the rising costs of health insurance, can make it extremely difficult for a GC to purchase health insurance and benefits. To make things easier on general contractors and their families, the Associated General Contractors (AGC) of America offers insurance help with their membership, called the AGC Alternative, which is a private insurance exchange where general contractors can shop for insurance for themselves, their employees, and their families.

The AGC Alternative website compares its exchange to Amazon.com, because its members can pick and choose from a broad range of health and other insurance benefits. There are a lot of benefits in obtaining health insurance from the AGC of America's program, with the biggest being the savings. AGC members receive a premium discount and thus save on complete health insurance plans that can include dental, vision, life, and disability in addition to legal service coverage. The discounts that a general contractor is eligible to receive will vary based on the number of employees that he or she has. In traditional health plans, the employer—in this case, the general contractor—is required to pay a percentage of every employee's premium, but with the AGC's program, the

GC pays into a defined contribution model. The defined contribution model is a set dollar amount charged per employee which is then used by the employee to purchase health insurance and other benefits from the private exchange. This is also beneficial to employees, as they're able to shop for their own coverage and potentially receive greater coverage than they previously had. Using this type of health coverage will also help general contractors retain current employees and hire new ones. Aside from annual salary, health benefits are extremely important, especially to those with families in a day and age where health insurance costs seem to always be on the rise. Best of all, the AGC's exchange program meets all of the minimum standards set forth by the Affordable Care Act (ACA), so employees can be confident that they're receiving equal coverage.

Speaking of the ACA, or its full title, the Patient Protection and Affordable Care Act (PPACA), it offers another option for general contractors in terms of health benefits and insurance. The PPACA is a US federal bill signed by President Barack Obama in March 2010 that helps to provide health insurance coverage to US residents. Its purpose is to provide quality, affordable health benefits to citizens while also helping to keep costs of insurance down for companies and the government.

As part of this act, US residents are able to browse the health insurance exchange and compare various coverage and policies offered by private insurance companies—similar to what the AGC offers to its members. The PPACA health insurance exchange is regulated by the government, and individuals who utilize these insurance plans with incomes between 100 percent and 400 percent of the federal poverty level are eligible to collect federal subsidies to help pay premium costs. While there are many different opinions on both the government and the PPACA health insurance offerings, the overarching goal is to provide low-cost insurance for those that need it. The exchange could be a useful resource for general contractors and others in the construction field.

Steady Rate of Growth

One of the most positive aspects of becoming a GC is that the field has seen rapid growth and is expected to continue to grow in coming years. According to the BLS, the job outlook, or the projected change in employment, for the construction industry is slated to increase 16 percent from 2012 to 2022, which is faster than other industries. The BLS states that there were roughly 485,000 jobs within the general contracting/construction management field in 2012. According to the BLS, an

The general contracting field has seen steady growth in the last few years, allowing for new jobs to be created.

increase of 11 percent during that same time period is the average among other industries. The general contracting field is one that's steadily growing. Also backing these claims is a report by the AGC of America, which states that 80 percent of firms polled plan on expanding their payrolls in 2015. The report surveyed more than nine hundred construction firms from forty-eight states and the District of Columbia. That same report also cited that industry growth expectations were set at 60 percent for

2015, and that 44 percent of firms planned on seeking projects outside of their traditional geographic locations.

The BLS further found that nonresidential construction made up nearly 25 percent of the 195,000 general contractor jobs in 2011, with those specific GCs earning $94,450 per year. The next statistic fully supports that the residential general contracting field can mean wealth, as they made up one-third of the job opportunities that year and earned $90,490 per year on average. It's worth noting that the highest-paying industry in 2011 was computer systems design, where workers in the field made an average of $136,770 per year.

As far as locations go, California and Texas provided the most job opportunities for general contractors in 2011, with 13 percent of all jobs coming from Texas, where GCs earned an average of $39.09 per hour, or $81,310 per year. California came in at 11 percent, where contractors brought home $107,760 annually, or $51.81 per hour. That trend remained the same in 2014, when Texas again ranked first in terms of employment for construction managers and GCs, paying them an average of $41.44 per hour, or $86,190, a $4,880 increase from three years before. California also came in second in 2014, as workers in the state saw an annual salary increase of $1,560, making $109,320 per year, or $52.56 per hour. In terms of the highest-paying state in 2011, that would be New York, where contractors earned an impressive $61.62 per hour, which translates into $128,170 for the year. New Jersey ranked second in terms of highest-paying states, where GCs earned an annual salary of $125,790, which breaks down to $60.48 per hour. That changed in 2014, however, as New Jersey became the highest-paying state for construction managers per the BLS' May 2014 data, when workers earned $63.05 per hour, which equates to $131,130 per year. That's $5,340 more than in 2011, and $6,580 more than the second-ranking state for 2014, which was Alaska, where workers earned $124,550 per year, or $59.88 per hour.

When you stop and think about it, it makes complete sense that the contracting and construction fields are continuing to grow. There are more people on the Earth than ever before—and that's only going to increase. There is a growing need for homes and buildings to provide shelter and workplaces for people. And since the average person doesn't have the required skills and training to build a home or design an office building, contractors and their teams are becoming more in demand. While it's true that shows on networks like HGTV and DIY make information on how to do this type of work more available to the general public, the fact remains that it takes much more than the information learned during a one-hour program to be able to do the type of work that a GC can do. Now, armed with that information, let's dig into the pros and cons of the job.

Pros & Cons

Like any job out there, there are both pros and cons to working as a general contractor. Let's get the cons over with first, because the general contracting field is one that's positive and rewarding as a whole. The first and

Despite television shows on channels like HGTV, a general contractor's expertise and connections will always be needed.

foremost negative aspect is the potential danger of the job. Since GCs work with dangerous tools, heavy equipment and machinery, and sometimes on buildings with multiple stories, there is some risk of injury, and the rate for work-related injuries is higher than average in the general contracting field. Next, the pressure of meeting deadlines can be a negative if you're the type of person who gets stressed easily or doesn't manage their time well. We've already learned that a good general contractor needs to be a solid project manager and stick to timelines, and when issues arise throughout the course of a project, it can be nerve-wracking for the GC. This career has the potential to create a lot of stress for a GC, which is definitely a con of the job. To go with that, the long hours that may come with the job can also be grueling.

Long hours are especially part of the deal when the general contractor is running his or her own business, as he or she is then tasked with a business owner's responsibilities in addition to making sure that the project gets completed on time for the homeowner. Also tying into this negative aspect of the job is the potential for travel and time spent away from family. Depending on how large of a project the general contractor is working on, they may have to travel long distances to a construction site. Another issue that general contractors sometimes have is that their prices are too high to be hired by homeowners, and thus they miss out on job opportunities. General contractors need to be careful with their pricing because they need to be able to make money on a project but still have competitive prices. Also while on the topic of missing out on job opportunities, GCs sometimes miss out on new work because they're currently tied up with another project. Since general contractors have to sign a contract with the homeowner, they're then locked into that specific job and are often unable to take on another one until the current project is complete.

Now let's examine all of the positives. As we just learned, one of the best reasons to enter the general contracting field is that it's a growing field, with 16 percent growth expected over the course of the next seven years or so. That type of growth isn't common in most fields, and that growth means job stability for a lot of GCs. Job stability is extremely important, especially for individuals with families who depend on a consistent paycheck. There are a lot of careers out there that don't provide the type of job security that the general contracting field does, so those looking to enter this type of career should keep this job benefit at the very top of the list. We've also learned that GCs can make a lot more money than most other careers. Of course, a career choice shouldn't be decided on salary alone, but it is an important deciding factor that can't be overlooked. Per 2014 data, an $86,270 average annual salary for a residential general contractor is much more than what the average person makes, thus making salary a huge benefit of the contracting field.

As we discussed earlier, a lot of general contractors work for themselves instead of for a firm. In fact, more than half of general contractors out there run their own

A general contractor's career can mean long hours, but it can also mean great pay, as the average annual salary for a residential contractor was $86,270 in 2014.

contracting businesses—57 percent to be exact—which is a benefit of the job if you want to run your own business. Owning your own professional construction business means that you're your own boss and don't have to answer to anyone but yourself. If you're the type of person who likes to make decisions and manage others, then that could be a positive for you in a GC's role. If you like being in a management role and overseeing others, then you'll like having subcontractors work for you. Also, in the case of owning your own business, you set your own hours and work as much or as little as possible. Of course, the GC needs to make sure the job gets done for the client, but the benefit is that it's on his or her terms. Owning your own construction company also means that your business expenses are tax-eligible. That means that expenses like trucks, tools, gas, office equipment, and anything else you use to run your business can be legally written off come tax season. Another pro of the job is that there are a variety of types of jobs that you can work on beyond just homes. Everything from office and government buildings to restaurants and schools are all projects that a general contractor can work on. In addition to that, the work of a GC isn't sedentary—a general contractor isn't stuck sitting inside at a desk from 9:00 to 5:00, five days a week. Additionally, they don't have to worry about having to spend each work day in an office with coworkers they may not get along with, or being stuck in long meetings. Instead, they're spending their time working outdoors and on their feet, staying active, and in most cases alongside individuals they've directly hired. Lastly, if a general contractor is licensed and has certain certifications, he or she can bid on larger projects and make more of a profit for their work.

Women in the General Contracting Field

While the construction industry as a whole is stereotypically dominated by men, women also play a major role in the general contracting field. That's evident in a blog post by Lowe's, a prominent home improvement chain store, which highlights five women who have found success working in the construction industry. Take Anna Stern, for example. Stern is the vice president of Tri-North Builders, a construction management company located in Wisconsin. She says that the biggest challenge she had to overcome was to prove to her coworkers that she had valuable thoughts and ideas to bring to the table. She also gave young women looking to break into the industry some advice, and that was to work in both the field and the office setting to get the most experience. Beverley Kruskol can also provide excellent insight and aspirations for young women looking to break into the general contracting field. Kruskol is the owner of M.Y. Pacific Building, a general contracting company based out of Los Angeles, California. She says that she's had to overcome contractors and other men on the construction site thinking that another male is the owner of her company, when in reality, it's Kruskol who's running the show. Her advice to young women looking to get started in the industry is to not be intimidated and to be assertive. The government has also taken strides to aid women in finding employment in the construction and general contracting industry. A public policy group called Women Impacting Public Policy partnered with American Express OPEN to launch what's called the Give Me Five initiative back in 2008. The goal is to provide female business owners with the information and knowledge to apply for federal contracting opportunities. Overall, women should not be overlooked in the general contracting field and should always be viewed as equals within the industry.

Tips For Getting Hired

Going to school, completing on-the-job training, and getting certified is only half the battle when it comes to obtaining a job in the general contracting field—you still need to put a cover letter and résumé together and find a company that's hiring. Full-time jobs may be easier to secure following an apprenticeship, but not all individuals are fortunate enough to find an apprenticeship that translates into an immediate career. A strong résumé for a general contractor will include his or her experience and skills within the field, but it also needs to be written in such a manner that's interesting and compelling. Anyone can list bullet points of their skills and experience, which is why you need to be creative in describing these things so that your résumé stands out in the eyes of the hiring manager. It should also be written so that hiring managers can clearly understand your value and worth to their companies. Another strong piece to a GC's résumé is the incorporation of a few references who can vouch for him or her, whether from a character standpoint or from past work experience. It's also important that you don't forget to include a cover letter to go with your résumé. Cover letters are a piece of the application process that applicants sometimes overlook. The purpose of the cover letter is to essentially sell yourself, detailing how your past experience, education, and character make you a great fit for the position.

When it comes to the job hunt itself, there are a lot of websites and job directories on the Internet that can serve as valuable tools for general contractors seeking work. Websites like Indeed, CareerBuilder, SimplyHired, Monster, and LinkedIn all have job postings within the general contracting and construction fields. There are also industry-specific job websites and directories, including ConstructionJobs.com, which was established in 2000 and provides job listings within the construction, design, and building industries.

The last step of the process is to secure an interview with a firm, agency, or private contractor. While the construction and general contracting fields are obviously ones that don't require you to wear a suit, it's crucial that interviewees dress well for the interview, wearing clean, ironed, and appropriate clothing. Before going to the interview, make sure your résumé is complete and that you know it like the back of your hand. You may want to even consider doing a mock interview with a family member or friend to prepare for the upcoming interview. It's also a good practice to read your résumé aloud to yourself, so that when you get into the interview, you don't have to keep looking down at your résumé for speaking points—you want to be able to speak confidently about your past experience and education, as well as the skills that you can bring to the company you're interviewing for.

ALTERNATIVE CAREERS TO GENERAL CONTRACTING

For those who are interested in becoming a general contractor, there are a lot of other, similar jobs that can serve as an alternative career, too. Entering a career in the construction field gives individuals the opportunity to learn multiple trades, and the skills that are acquired are invaluable, careerwise. And because of that, there are a lot of alternate careers that can keep a person working in construction, just not in a management position like that of a general contractor. One alternative career is a cost estimator, who's responsible for studying blueprints in order to establish cost estimates for a project. Cost estimators work with architects, general contractors, and other construction members to review project information and analyze areas that could save both time and money. Cost estimators should work well with numbers and be able to make accurate projections on a construction site. To become a cost estimator, a bachelor's degree is usually required, but the good news is that it's a growing field. The BLS reports that the cost estimator field is predicted to rise by 26 percent between now and 2022. While cost estimators don't earn as high of a salary as GCs, their median salary comes in around $58,860.

Another alternative career path to a general contractor is to become an architect. It's important to note that becoming an architect is just as involved as choosing to be a GC, because architects need to be licensed, complete an architecture program, pass an exam, and have some on-the-job experience to be hired. The main role that an architect plays on a construction site is designing the build, consulting with the client, and visiting the worksite and checking in with the general contractor and his or her team. Today, many architects are using technology and computer software to mock up designs, so it's important that an architect learns and stays up to date on the latest technologies available in the field. Architecture is also a growing field—at 17 percent through 2022—and architects earned an average annual salary of $73,090 for individuals not working in the landscape or naval categories in 2012. For those interested in doing a lot of hands-on labor, you may want to consider becoming a subcontractor who would work under the direct supervision of the general contractor. Maybe a supervising role and project management isn't for you, but you can pursue a career as a sub in a construction-specific field like plumbing, electrical, or bricklaying. This way, you're still playing a crucial role in the project but don't have to deal with the day-to-day tasks that a general contractor does.

If a career as a general contractor doesn't work out, becoming a designer or architect can be a great alternative.

By now it should be clear that there are multiple benefits to choosing a career as a general contractor, but that there's also a lot of hard work that goes into the career. A budding GC must have certain interests and become acquainted with the field. Then there's all of the schooling, courses, and on-the-job training that's required to get an "in" in the field. From there, more field experience is necessary for a general contractor to fully understand all aspects of the trade. It's important to remember that GCs aren't just awarded this type of management position right out of school. They start out in a specific trade and then work their way up to become a general contractor, where they're responsible for all aspects of the construction site. Due to all of the responsibility that's put on a general contractor's shoulders, they're paid higher than the average employee in other industries, and it's well deserved. Additionally, general contractors will always be needed since the average homeowner isn't expected to conduct major construction, and given the projected growth rate of the general contracting and construction field, it proves that entering this career would be a great choice for anyone.

Glossary

apprenticeship A form of post-secondary training that typically encompasses both classroom learning and on-the-job training within a service industry.

architect Also known as a designer or engineer, an architect plans the design of the building and then works with the general contractor and his or her team to assure that the building is built to the design plans.

authority having jurisdiction (AHJ) An agency that has the authority to provide official inspections and approval for a job based on health, safety, and public welfare.

bid bond A bond that assures that an owner doesn't pay more for a project than what was agreed upon by the winning bid of a contractor.

capacity One of the three main areas that surety companies look at when deciding if a general contractor meets the requirements to purchase a surety bond, capacity refers to a contractor's qualification and skill set to be able to understand the scope of work and complete a project from start to finish. A general contractor's years of experience, past work history, amount of work currently on their plate, and organization and management are all factored into the determination of their capacity.

capital One of the three main areas that surety companies look at when deciding if a general contractor meets the requirements to purchase a surety bond, capital refers to the amount of money that the general contractor has, which also translates into his or her ability to be able to finance a project, which includes being able to pay for subcontractors and suppliers.

certificate of occupancy A document issued by the AHJ that states that a building meets all requirements and can be occupied.

character One of the three main areas that surety companies look at when deciding if a general contractor meets the requirements to purchase a surety bond, character refers to the integrity of a general contractor or company he or she is employed by.

demobilization The removal of all trailers, heavy machinery, tools, and other supplies from a construction site once the project has been completed.

first-tier subcontractor A contractor who specializes in a specific area of construction who may also hire subcontractors to work under him or her.

mobilization The act of moving all trailers, heavy machinery, tools, and other supplies onto a construction site so that a project can begin.

payment bond A bond that assures homeowners that any subcontractors or suppliers that assisted in a project will get paid by the general contractor.

performance bond A construction bond that assures a homeowner that the scope of work that was agreed upon at the price of the bid will be completed.

permit A document issued by an authority having jurisdiction that gives the authorization to begin a project that meets regulatory requirements.

preconstruction The period between the awarding of construction and construction actually beginning.

second-tier subcontractor A contractor that's hired by a subcontractor who provides specialty work on a construction project.

subcontractor A specialty trade contractor that's hired by a general contractor to provide work on a construction project.

supplier A company or individual that manufactures or supplies products and services to a contractor for a construction project.

surety A company—often an insurance company—that sells construction bonds to contractors.

surety bond Also known as a construction bond, a surety bond helps homeowners measure risk management and potential issues with a general contractor or his or her work.

Further Information

Books

Egan, Joe. *The General Contractor: How to Be a Great Success or Failure*. Plymouth, MN: Egan Publications, 2012.

Fatu, Claudiu. *Starting Your Career as a Contractor: How to Build and Run a Construction Business*. New York: Allworth Press, 2015.

Ganaway, Nick. *Construction Business Management: What Every Construction Contractor, Builder & Subcontractor Needs To Know*. Rockland, MA: RSMeans, 2006.

Websites

Associated General Contractors of America
www.agc.org
The AGC is the United States' largest association serving the construction industry,

Construction Management Association of America
www.cmaanet.org
The CMAA was founded in 1982 and is the only association dedicated to construction management professionals.

Study.com: Becoming a General Contractor:
study.com/becoming_a_general_contractor.html
Visit this website for a detailed overview on the necessary steps to becoming a general contractor.

Bibliography

American Institute of Construction. "About the AIC." http://www.professionalconstructor.org/?page=About.

Angie's List. "Guide to licensed, bonded & insured contractors." http://www.angieslist.com/contractor/license-bonded-insured.htm.

Angie's List. "Guide to signing a contract." http://www.angieslist.com/contractor/signing-a-contract.htm.

Angie's List. "Guide to working with contractors." http://www.angieslist.com/contractor/working-with-contractors.htm.

The Associated General Contractors of America. "Eighty Percent of Construction Firms Plan to Expand Headcount in 2015 as Contractors Foresee Growing Demand in Most Market Sectors." https://www.agc.org/eighty-percent-construction-firms-plan-expand-headcount-2015-contractors-foresee-growing-demand-most.

The Associated General Contractors of America. "Private Insurance Exchange." http://alternative.agc.org/.

Carr, Karen. "History of Houses." http://www.historyforkids.org/learn/architecture/houses.htm.

Construction Management Association of America. "Becoming a CCM." http://cmaanet.org/becoming-ccm.

Dodge Data & Analytics. "Construction Industry to See More Balanced Growth in 2015 According to Dodge Data & Analytics. http://construction.com/about-us/press/construction-industry-to-see-more-balanced-growth-in-2015-according-to-DDG.asp.

Dykstra, Alison. *Construction Project Management: A Complete Introduction*. Santa Rosa, CA: Kirschner Publishing, 2011.

General Contractor License Guide. "How to Become a Licensed Contractor." http://generalcontractorlicenseguide.com/.

House Building Careers. "The History of House Building." http://housebuildingcareers.org.uk/history-of-house-building.

IECRM.org. "Live-Online Electrical Apprenticeship Program." http://www.iecrm.org/education-and-training/live-online-electrical-apprentice-training/.

Joyner, Jeffrey. "Job Description of General Contractors." http://work.chron.com/job-description-general-contractors-12435.html.

Learn.org. "How to Become a General Contractor in 5 Steps." http://learn.org/articles/General_Contractor_5_Steps_to_Becoming_a_General_Contractor.html.

Learn How to Become. "How to Become a Contractor: Careers in Contracting." http://www.learnhowtobecome.org/contractor/.

LearningPath.org. "Becoming a General Contractor: Job Description & Salary Information." http://learningpath.org/articles/General_Contractor_Career_Summary.html.

Locsin, Aurelio. "The Average Salary of a General Contractor." http://work.chron.com/average-salary-general-contractor-6862.html.

Lowe's. How 5 Women Have Found Success in the Construction Industry." https://www.lowesforpros.com/articles/how-5-women-have-found-success-in-the-construction-industry_a1476.html.

MacLoone, Sharon. "New Program Educates Women on Contracting Opportunities." http://voices.washingtonpost.com/small-business/2008/10/new_program_educates_women_on.html.

OSHA. "Women in Construction." https://www.osha.gov/doc/topics/women/.

San Diego AGC Apprenticeship & Training Trust. "Apprentice Information." http://www.agcsdatt.org/apprentice_information.

Study.com. "Education Requirements for a General Contractor License." http://study.com/articles/General_Contractor_Educational_Requirements_for_a_Contractors_License.html.

Study.com. "General Contractor: Job Outlook & Career Requirements." http://study.com/articles/General_Contractor_Job_Outlook_and_Requirements_for_a_Career_in_General_Contracting.html.

Study.com. "How to Become a General Contractor." http://study.com/how_to_become_a_general_contractor.html.

Study.com. "Requirements to Becoming a General Contractor." http://study.com/becoming_a_general_contractor.html.

United States Department of Labor. "Affordable Care Act." http://www.dol.gov/ebsa/healthreform/.

United States Department of Labor, Bureau of Labor Statistics. "Occupational Employment Statistics: Occupational Employment and Wages, May 2014, Construction Managers." http://www.bls.gov/oes/current/oes119021.htm.

United States Department of Labor, Bureau of Labor Statistics. "Occupational Outlook Handbook: Construction Managers." http://www.bls.gov/ooh/management/construction-managers.htm#tab-1.

Wermiel, Sara. "Norcross, Fuller, and the Rise of the General Contractor in the United States in the Nineteenth Century." http://www.arct.cam.ac.uk/Downloads/ichs/vol-3-3297-3314-wermiel.pdf.

Index

Page numbers in **boldface** are illustrations. Entries in **boldface** are glossary terms.

About the Author

Pete Schauer is a freelance writer from East Windsor, New Jersey. He holds a BA in English Writing Concentration and an MA in Professional Communication from William Paterson University, and currently serves as the digital marketing manager at SEMGeeks, a digital marketing and web design/development agency. In his spare time, Pete enjoys writing, sports, and spending time with his wife, Liz, and dog, Toby.